MW00805053

Held In Heaven's Hand

by
Hannah Grace

AuthorHouse™
1663 Liberty Drive, Suite 200
Bloomington, IN 47403
www.authorhouse.com
Phone: 1-800-839-8640

First published by AuthorHouse 1/5/2009

ISBN: 978-1-4259-2498-0 (sc)

Library of Congress Control Number: 2006906173

Printed in the United States of America
Bloomington, Indiana

This book is printed on acid-free paper.

authorHOUSE®

This is written in loving memory of:

Name:_____

Date:_____

Attach picture here.

He will wipe every tear from your eye.
Revelation 21-4

My dear friend, may these words offer you comfort in your time of grief. You are in my prayers and thoughts. May His love hold you always.

With much love,
Hannah Grace

Acknowledgements

I want to acknowledge God for continuing to give me the words to write for those in need of His love and comfort. I also want to acknowledge my church home family who continues to support me in these endeavors with prayer, friendship, and encouragement.

Dedication

I lovingly dedicate this book to the families in whom these words will be a source of hope and comfort.

It is my prayer that the message in this book will touch your heart and comfort you at this time. May his love surround you and your family and may you feel His presence always...

You see your friend in much pain and sadness.

No medicine seems to make them well, and they hurt all over.

So now, you look at me with such a saddened face and tears that fall.

Your heart aches for this sweet friend, whose life has been one hurt after another.

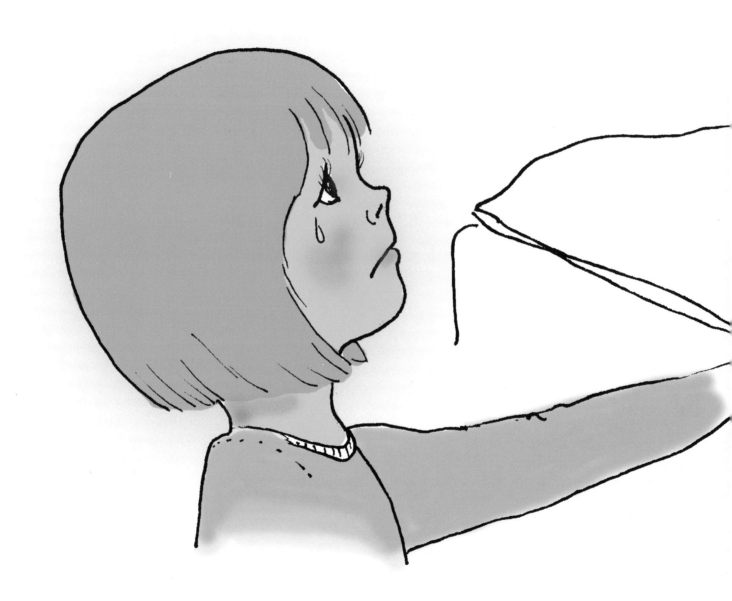

Let me tell you, they are in a place where their hurting is all gone.

No medicine is ever needed. There are no tears of sadness or pain.

God loves His precious children, so He sends His angels from above to watch over them.

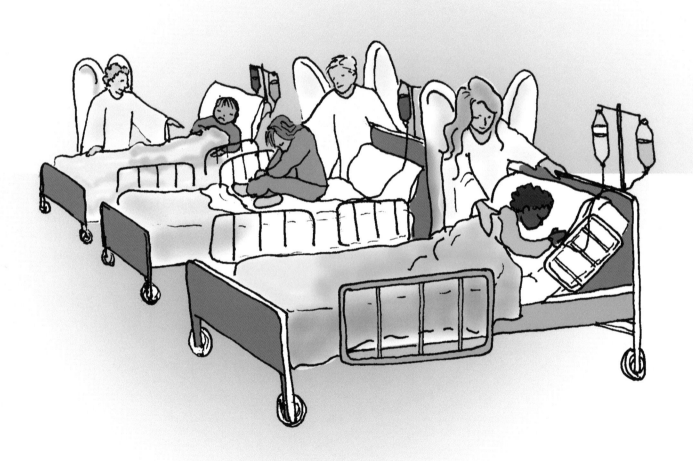

Yet He also knows that sometimes they are too sick and won't get well, so He takes them home to Heaven's Wonderland to be with Him.

So He gently tells their angels, who are always watching with tenderness, what to do.

When their life carries too much pain, and no bandage ever makes it better;
God will gently carry them home to Heaven.

There are no tears where they are now, only smiles and the ability to play;
Dancing with angels as they sing to them sweet lullabies of kindness.

It is a place where there is no hurting, and though we don't see them,
They are now playing on God's playground above the sun...

At nighttime, you can look above the stars,
which glimmer and shine,
And wonder if they are dangling them for you
with love.

When the clouds make their shapes in the sky,
maybe angels and children
Prance and play above them, making fun
shapes for your delight.

I know you will be sad for awhile, and that is okay; for tears are normal when we lose someone (a grandmother, a son, or a friend) we love and hold their time on earth with us close in our heart.

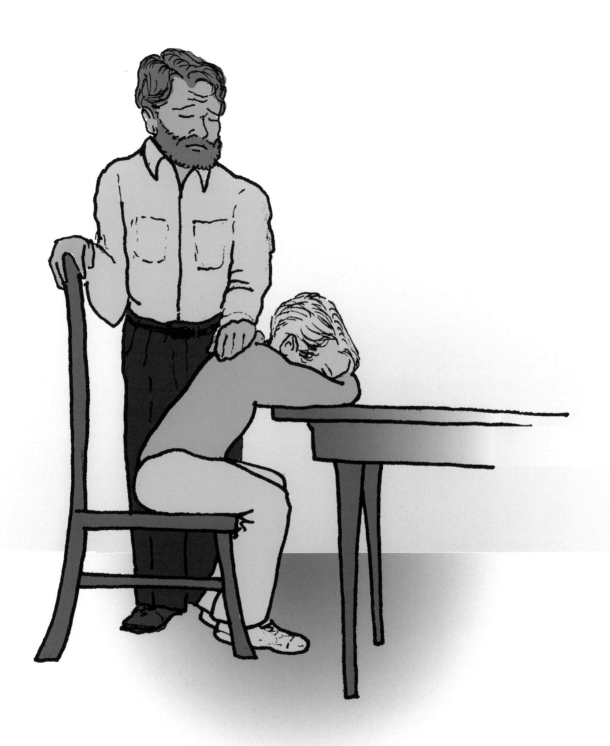

Let me wipe those tender tears from your eyes and share my thoughts.

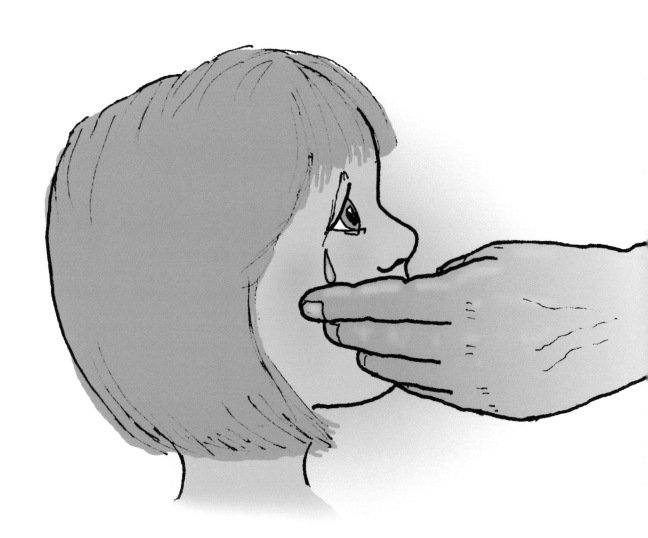

For these precious children are called by their name, and God, our Father, will
Hold them gently in Heaven's hand today, tomorrow, and always.

About the Author

The author, Hannah Grace, resides near the nation's capitol.

I enjoy writing and have been since I was a child.

I also enjoy horseback riding and playing tennis and reading.

My prayer is that the words in the books that God is allowing me to write will be of help to families in times of need. I pray that the life God has given me and the words that I write will be of help to others and will touch their hearts and draw them closer to Christ because of them. You are precious and you are loved by an Almighty God who loves you with an everlasting love.

Printed in the United States
149460LV00002B